DRUM
RECORDED VERSIONS

RED HOT CHILI P...

NOTE - FOR - NOTE
TRANSCRIPTIONS

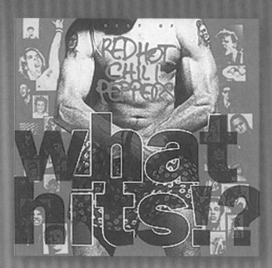

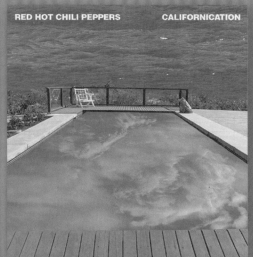

Music Transcriptions by Scott Schroedl

ISBN 0-634-05275-6

HAL•LEONARD®
CORPORATION
7777 W. BLUEMOUND RD. P.O. BOX 13819 MILWAUKEE, WI 53213

Visit Hal Leonard Online at
www.halleonard.com

In Australia Contact:
Hal Leonard Australia Pty. Ltd.
22 Taunton Drive P.O. Box 5130
Cheltenham East, 3192 Victoria, Australia
Email: ausadmin@halleonard.com

CONTENTS

4   AEROPLANE

11   BREAKING THE GIRL

19   BY THE WAY

25   CALIFORNICATION

33   GET UP AND JUMP

40   GIVE IT AWAY

46   GOOD TIME BOYS

54   HIGHER GROUND

60   KNOCK ME DOWN

67   ME AND MY FRIENDS

74   MELLOWSHIP SLINKY IN B MAJOR

82   MINOR THING

88   MY FRIENDS

92   NOBODY WEIRD LIKE ME

101   ONE BIG MOB

110   RIGHT ON TIME

115   SCAR TISSUE

122   THROW AWAY YOUR TELEVISION

127   TRUE MEN DON'T KILL COYOTES

136   UNDER THE BRIDGE

141   DRUM NOTATION LEGEND

from *One Hot Minute*

Aeroplane

Words and Music by Anthony Kiedis, Flea, Chad Smith and David Navarro

that moth-er - fuck-er's al - ways spiked __ with pain. 1. A -

Verse

look-ing in __ my own __ eyes, _____ hel - lo, ___ I can find the love I want. __

__ Some-one bet-ter slap me be-fore I start to

rust, be-fore I start to de-com - pose. _ Look-ing in my rear - view mir -

ror. Look-ing in my rear - view mir - ror, ___

I can make it dis-ap-pear. _ I can make it dis-ap-

Chorus

pear, have no fear. I like pleas-ure spiked _ with pain and mu-sic is my aer-o-plane,

it's my aer - o - plane. Song-bird sweet and sour Jane, and

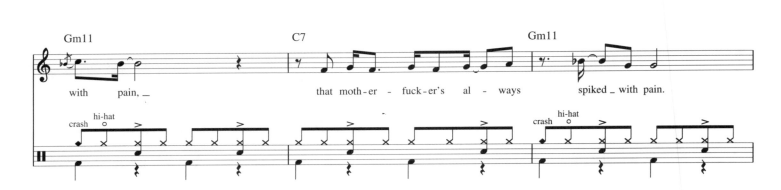

mu-sic is my aer-o-plane, it's my aer-o-plane. Pleas-ure _ spiked

with pain, _ that moth-er-fuck-er's al-ways spiked _ with pain.

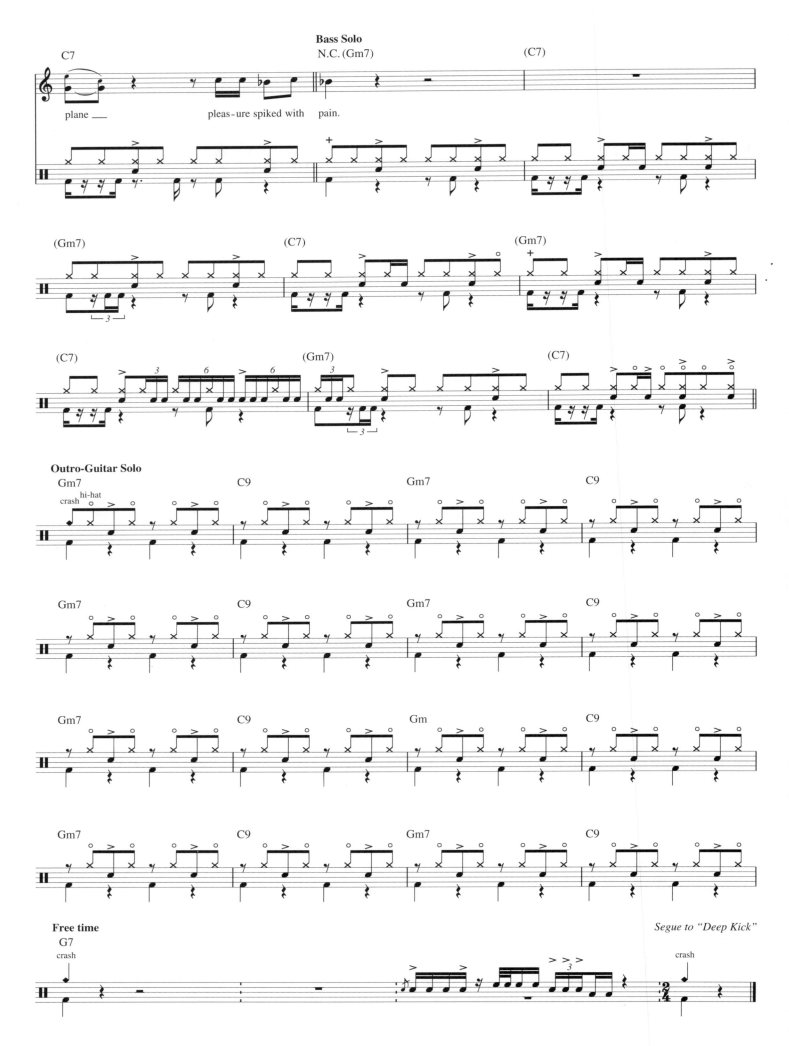

from *Blood Sugar Sex Magik*

Breaking the Girl

Words and Music by Anthony Kiedis, Flea, John Frusciante and Chad Smith

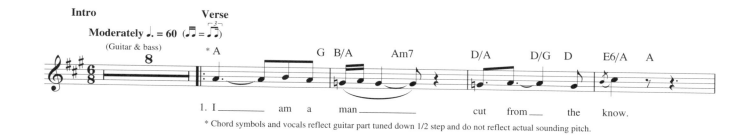

1. I _____ am a man _____ cut from _____ the know.

* Chord symbols and vocals reflect guitar part tuned down 1/2 step and do not reflect actual sounding pitch.

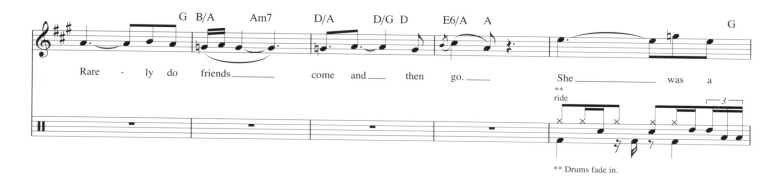

Rare - ly do friends _____ come and _____ then go. _____ She _____ was a

** ride

** Drums fade in.

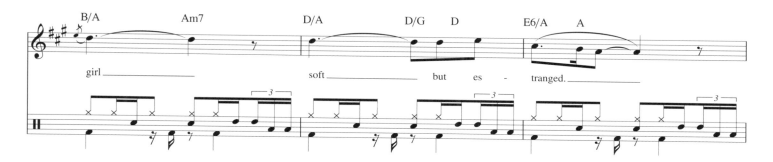

girl _____ soft _____ but es - tranged. _____

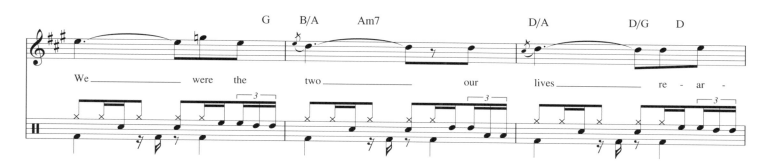

We _____ were the two _____ our lives _____ re - ar -

ranged. _____

crash ride

Feel - ing so

He loves no _____ one else.

Interlude

Chorus

Play 7 times

Twist-ing and turn-ing, your feel-ings are burn-ing, you're break-ing the girl. _____

She meant you _____ no harm.

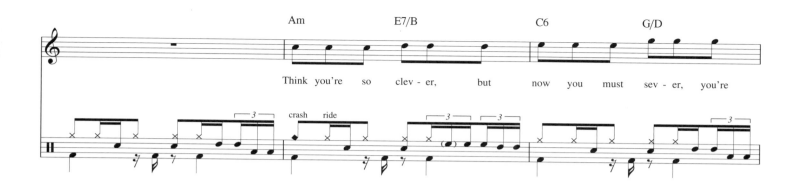

Think you're so clev- er, but now you must sev- er, you're

break-ing the girl. _____ He loves

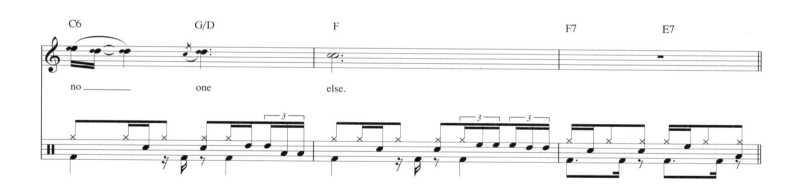

no _____ one else.

Outro

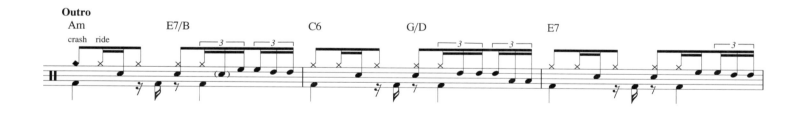

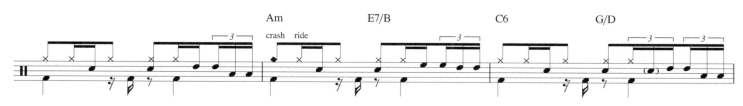

Begin fade

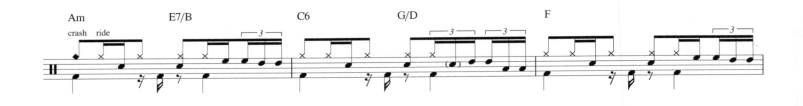

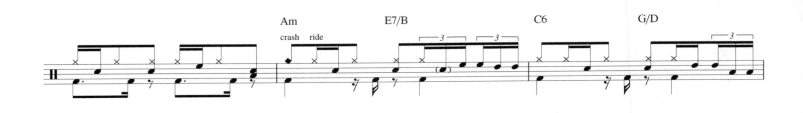

Fade out

from *By the Way*

By the Way

Words and Music by Anthony Kiedis, Flea, John Frusciante and Chad Smith

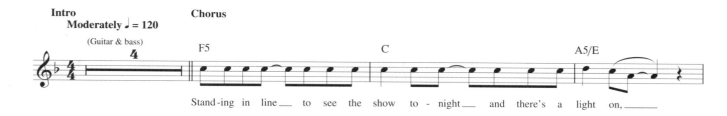

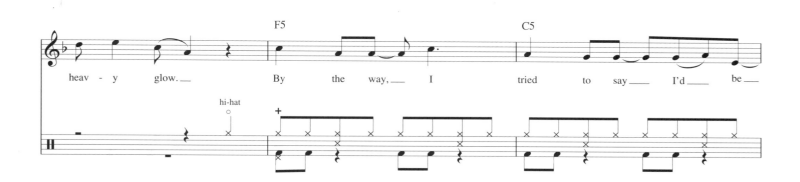

Standing in line to see the show tonight and there's a light on,

heavy glow. By the way, I tried to say I'd be

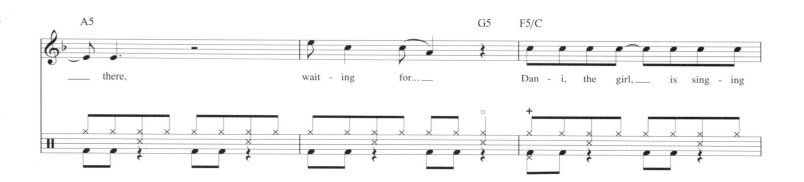

there, waiting for... Dani, the girl, is singing

songs to me beneath the marquee, overload.

Interlude
Dm
crash

show to-night __ and there's a light on, _____ heav-y glow. __

By the way, __ I tried to say __ I'd __ be __ there, wait - ing for... __
(Oh.) _____

Interlude

Verse

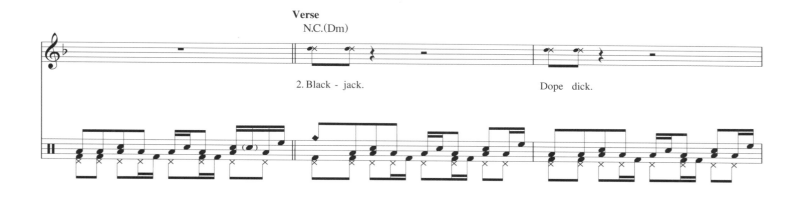

2. Black - jack.   Dope dick.

Pawn shop.   Quick pick.   Kiss that dyke, I know __ you want to hold one.

Not on strike, but I'm a - bout to bowl one. Bite that mic, I know you nev - er stole one.

Girls that like a sto - ry, so I told one. Song - bird. Main line.

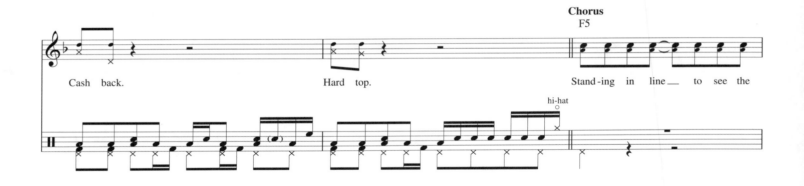

Chorus
F5

Cash back. Hard top. Stand-ing in line to see the

hi-hat

C/E   A5   F5

show to - night and there's a light on, heav - y glow. By the way, I

C5   A5/E   F5

tried to say I'd be there, wait - ing for... Dan - i, the girl, is sing - ing

from *Californication*

Californication

Words and Music by Anthony Kiedis, Flea, John Frusciante and Chad Smith

25

Verse

2. It's the edge of the world and all of wes-tern civ-'li-za-tion; the

sun may rise in the east, at least it's set-tled, in the fin-al lo-ca-tion. It's

un-der-stood that Hol-ly-wood sells Cal-i-for-ni-ca-tion.

Pre-Chorus

Bkgd. Voc.: w/ Voc. Fig. 1, (4 times)

Pay your sur-geon ver-y well to break the spell of a-ging. Ce-

crash ride

Voc. Fig. 1

(Ooh.)

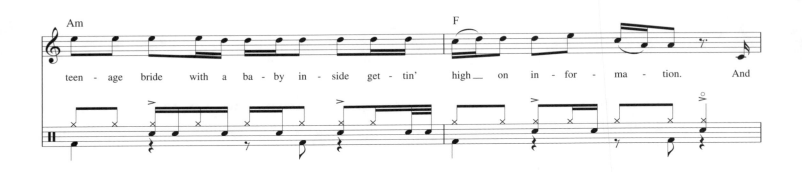

teen - age bride with a ba - by in - side get - tin' high __ on in - for - ma - tion. And

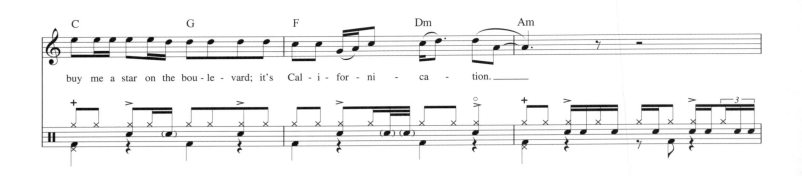

buy me a star on the bou - le - vard; it's Cal - i - for - ni - ca - tion. _____

Verse

4. Space may be the fin - al fron - tier, but it's made in a Hol - ly - wood base - ment. And

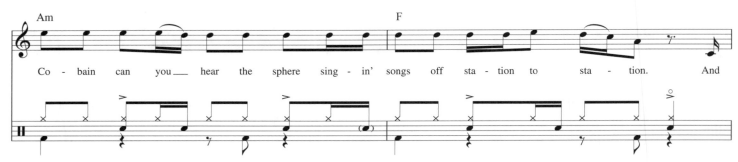

Co - bain can you __ hear the sphere sing - in' songs off sta - tion to sta - tion. And

from *What Hits!?*

Get Up and Jump

Words and Music by Flea and Anthony Kiedis

Intro
Moderate Funk ♩ = 130

Rap: 1. A - get up an' jump, a - get up an' jump. A get up, get up, get up an' jump. A - jump on up a - jump on down, just jump - a, jump - a, jump - a, jump - a, jump a - round. Jump the day a - way, jump all o - ver town 'cause

jump-in's o - kay in a jump-in' kind-a way. Hey, hey.

Jump-a

boy, jump - a girl, jump - a rope, jump for joy. Just don't___ stop jump - in, keep your heart mus - cle pump - in'.

Hill - el be jump - in' on that lit - tle ba - by Frump-kin. Say, what you got, a pump-kin in your pants?

When you're just stand - in' or sit - tin' still, ___

think a - bout the frogs get - tin' a thrill. ___ Take a lit - tle les - son from the kan - ga - roos, ___ a

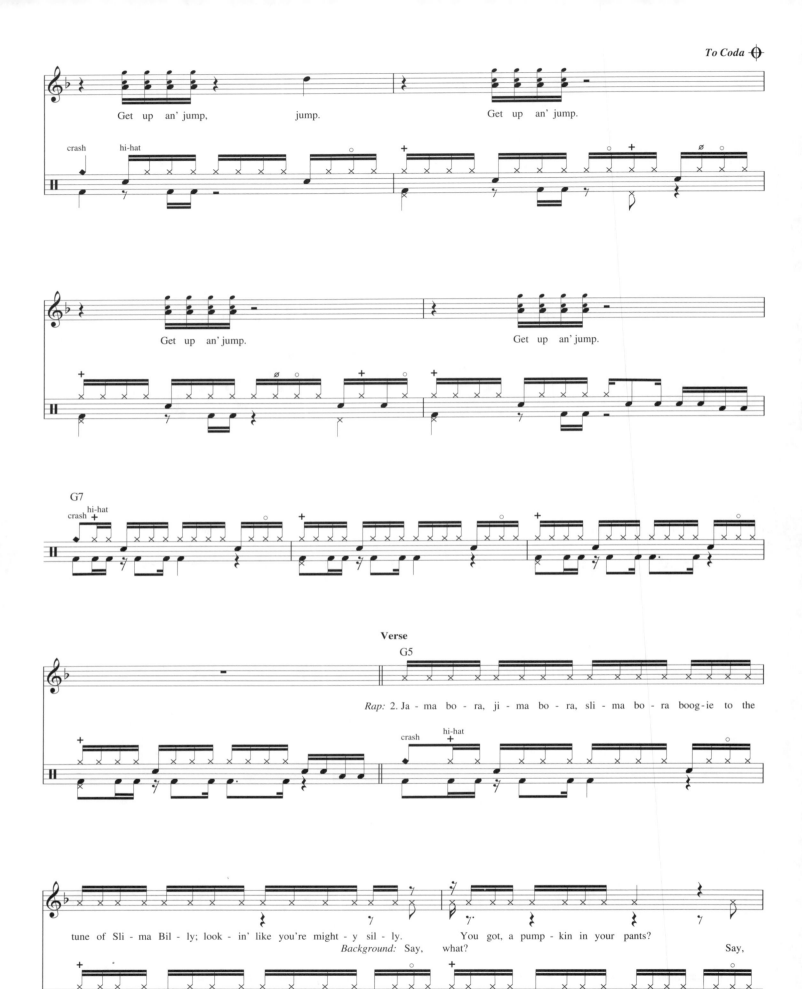

Get up an' jump, jump. Get up an' jump.

Get up an' jump. Get up an' jump.

Verse

Rap: 2. Ja - ma bo - ra, ji - ma bo - ra, sli - ma bo - ra boog - ie to the

tune of Sli - ma Bil - ly; look - in' like you're might - y sil - ly. You got, a pump - kin in your pants?

Background: Say, what? Say,

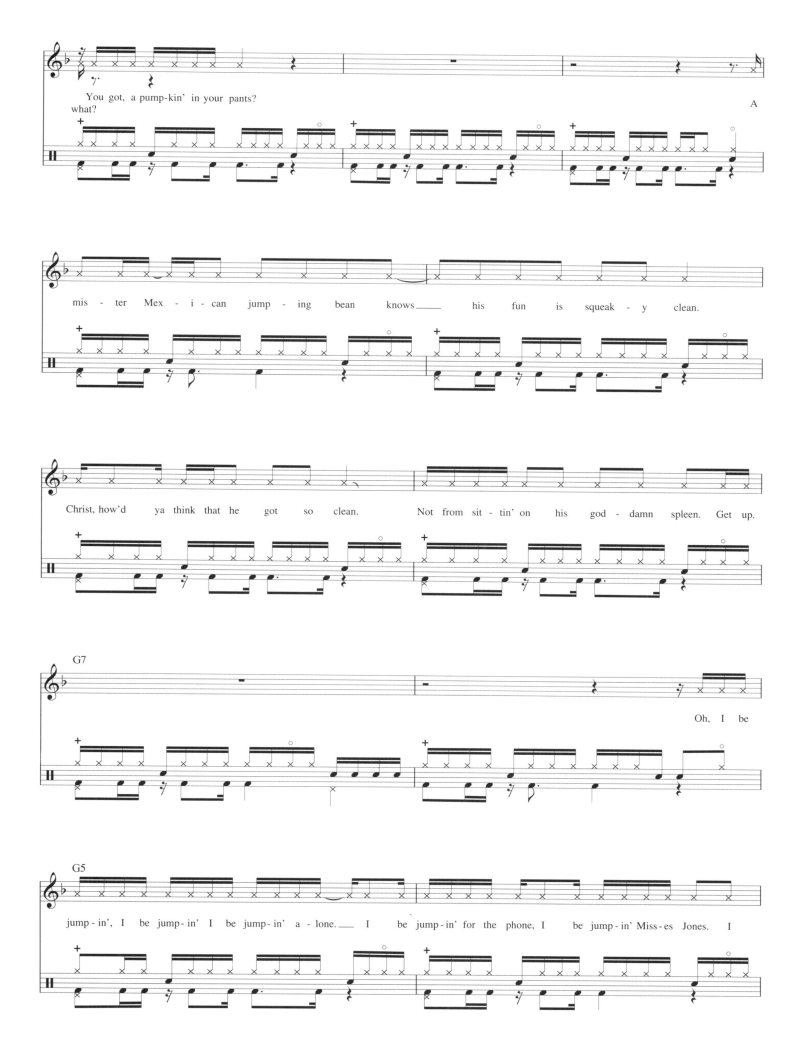

You got, a pump-kin' in your pants?
what?

A

mis - ter Mex - i - can jump - ing bean knows_____ his fun is squeak - y clean.

Christ, how'd ya think that he got so clean. Not from sit - tin' on his god - damn spleen. Get up.

G7

Oh, I be

G5

jump - in', I be jump - in' I be jump - in' a - lone.____ I be jump - in' for the phone, I be jump - in' Miss - es Jones. I

Verse

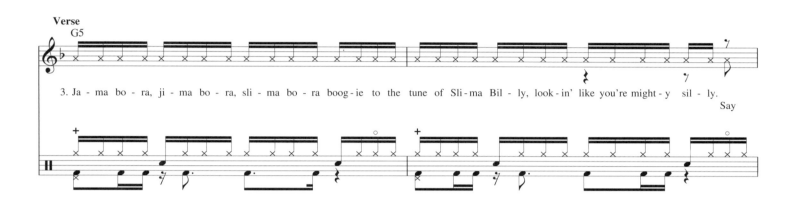

3. Ja - ma bo - ra, ji - ma bo - ra, sli - ma bo - ra boog - ie to the tune of Sli - ma Bil - ly, look - in' like you're might - y sil - ly. Say

You got a pump-kin in your pants?   You got, a pump-kin' in your pants?
what?   Say, what?

Outro

from *Blood Sugar Sex Magik*

Give It Away

Words and Music by Anthony Kiedis, Flea, John Frusciante and Chad Smith

I can't tell if I'm a king-pin or a pau-per! Oh, oh, yeah! —

Give it a-way, give it a-way, give it a-way now. — Give it a-way, give it a-way, give it a-way now. —

Give it a-way, give it a-way, give it a-way now. — I can't tell if I'm a king-pin or a pau-per! —

Guitar Solo

D.S. al Coda 1

Bm B♭m Am A♭m Gm F♯m Fm Em E♭m Dm C♯m Cm

3. Look at

Coda 1

Chorus

A5

Give it a-way, give it a-way, give it a-way now.___ Give it a-way, give it a-way, give it a-way now.___

Give it a-way, give it a-way, give it a-way now.___ I can't tell if I'm a king-pin or a pau-per!

Guitar Solo

D.S. al Coda 2

✵ Coda 2
Outro-Chorus

Give it a-way, give it a-way, give it a-way now.___ Give it a-way, give it a-way, give it a-way now.___

Give it a-way, give it a-way, give it a-way now.___ Give it a-way, give it a-way, give it a-way now.___

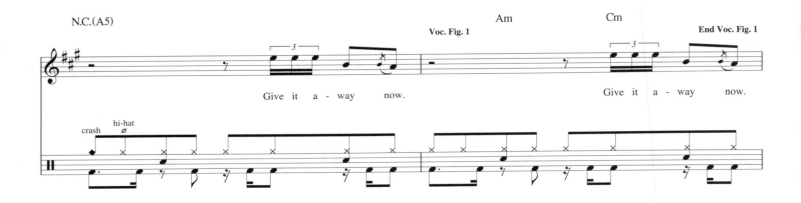

Give it a-way now. Give it a-way now.

w/ Voc. Fig. 1 (18 times)

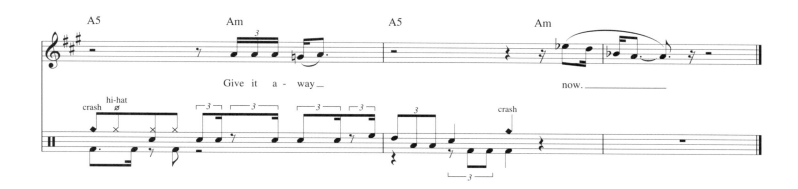

Additional Lyrics

3. Lucky me, swimmin' in my ability,
   Dancin' down on life with agility.
   Come and drink it up from my fertility,
   Blessed with a bucket of lucky mobility.
   My mom, I love her 'cause she love me,
   Long gone are the times when she scrub me.
   Feelin' good, my brother gonna hug me,
   Drink up my juice, young love, chug-a-lug me.
   There's a river born to be a giver,
   Keep you warm, won't let you shiver.
   His heart is never gonna wither,
   Come on everybody, time to deliver.

from *Mother's Milk*

Good Time Boys

Words and Music by Anthony Kiedis, Flea, John Frusciante and Chad Smith

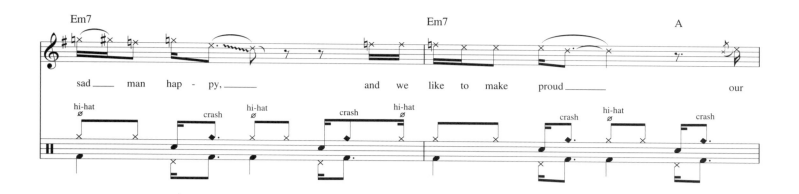

sad___ man hap-py,___ and we like to make proud___ our

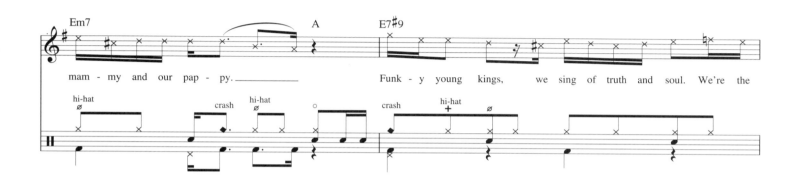

mam-my and our pap-py.___ Funk-y young kings, we sing of truth and soul. We're the

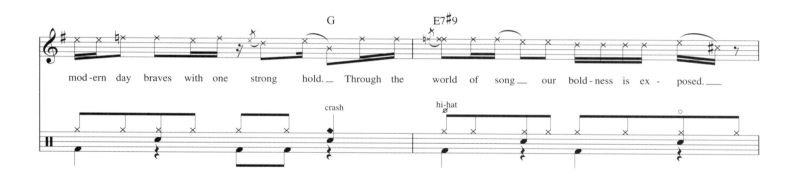

mod-ern day braves with one strong hold.___ Through the world of song___ our bold-ness is ex-posed.___

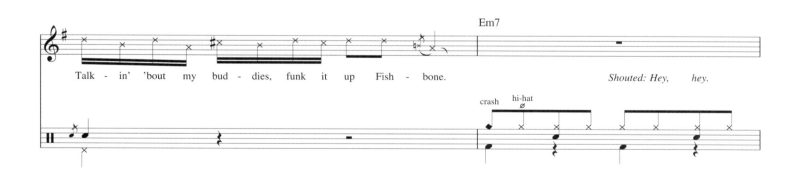

Talk-in' 'bout my bud-dies, funk it up Fish-bone. *Shouted: Hey, hey.*

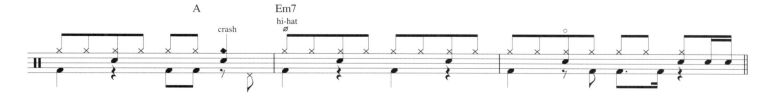

Chorus

Good, good time __ boys, make me feel __ good.

Give me good __ times, yea, yea, _____ yea, yea. _____ Good, good time __ boys,

make me feel __ good. Give me good __ times, yea, yea, _____ yea, yea. _____

Free Time
N.C.

Spoken: *Got me bonin'...

A Tempo

Interlude
Gm

*w/ misc. samples from Fishbone, Thelonius Monster, & FIREHOUSE recordings (approx. 10 sec.)

build-ing up our brains___ with su - per - nat - u - ral pow - ers, we take it from the trees___ and the Might - y Watts Tow - ers.

Aim the flame of free - dom at the lames and sours, we're the best of the West and the West is ours.

Chorus

Good, good time___ boys, make me feel___ good.

Give me good___ times, yea, yea,_____ yea, yea.___ Good, good time___ boys,

make me feel_ good. Give me good___ times, yea, yea,_____ yea, yea.

from *Mother's Milk*

Higher Ground

Words and Music by Stevie Wonder

from *Mother's Milk*

Knock Me Down

Words and Music by Anthony Kiedis, Flea, John Frusciante and Chad Smith

Verse

2. I'm tired of be - in' un - touch - a - ble, _____ I'm not a - bove the love. _____

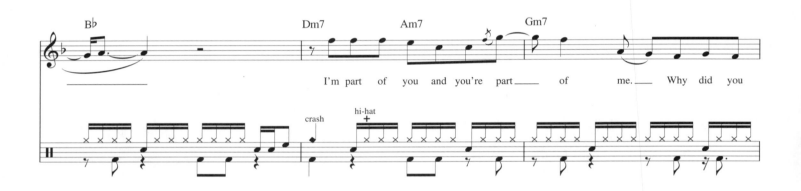

_____ I'm part of you and you're part _____ of me. _____ Why did you

Bridge

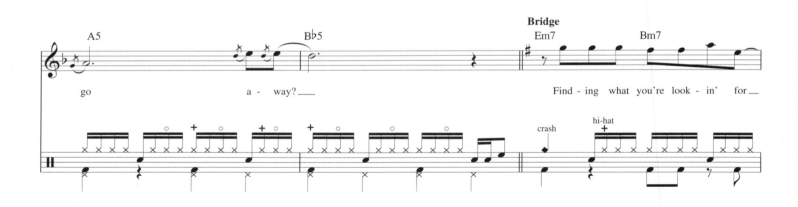

go a - way? _____ Find - ing what you're look - in' for _____

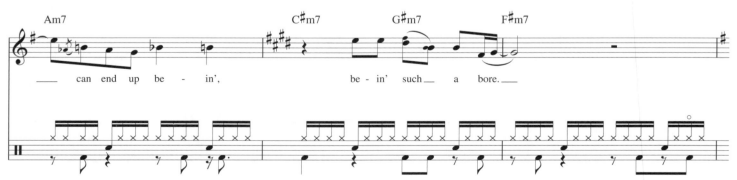

_____ can end up be - in', be - in' such a bore. _____

from *What Hits!?*

Me and My Friends

Words and Music by Flea, Anthony Kiedis, Hillel Slovak and Jack Irons

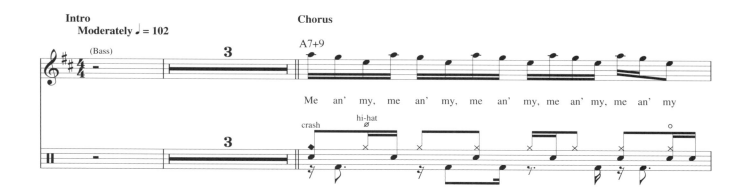

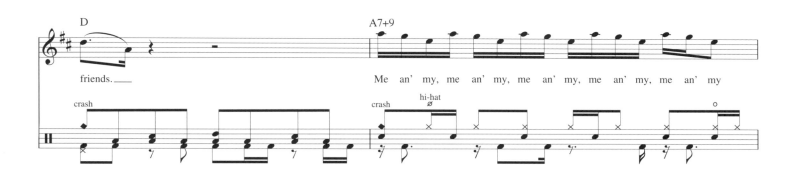

Chorus

Me an' my, me an' my, me an' my, me an' my, me an' my

friends. _____

Me an' my, me an' my, me an' my, me an' my, me an' my

friends. _____

Guitar Solo
N.C.

Spoken: 3. (A) Jack - y's eyes are closed — but he's right on course be - cause he's

guid - ed by — the in - vis - i - ble force. — He drives a kook - y green Chrys - ler, bad as an - y - bod - y's Porsche. He's a

work - ing class drum - mer, he's as strong as a horse. —   Me an' my, me an' my, me an' my, me an' my, me an' my

72

friends. _____

Me an' my, me an' my, me an' my, me an' my, me an' my

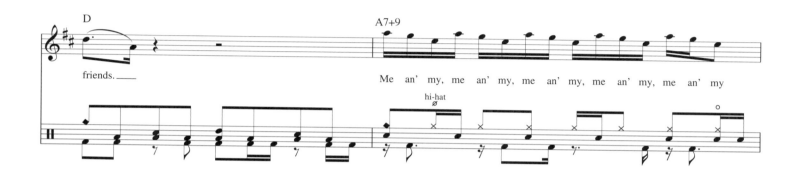

friends. _____

Me an' my, me an' my, me an' my, me an' my, me an' my

friends. _____

Me an' my, me an' my, me an' my, me an' my, me an' my

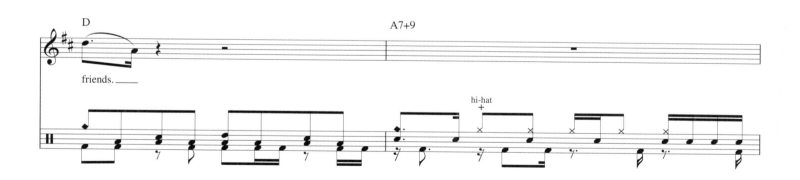

friends. _____

from *Blood Sugar Sex Magik*
Mellowship Slinky in B Major
Words and Music by Anthony Kiedis, Flea, John Frusciante and Chad Smith

a thun -der storm and a man like Ty - son. Pop - corn, pea - nuts, look-in' at big butts,

no I can - not keep my mouth shut. Rock-in' to the beat of the fab - u - lous Fo - rum,

my La - kers, I a - dore 'em. Blush my la - dy when I tell her

that I do in - deed love to smell her. Sop - ping wet your pink um - brel - la,

I do the dog with Is - a - bel - la.
(Do _____ the dog _____ with Is - a - bel - la.

Chorus

I'm so in love, yes, with an ar-tist, i-mag-i-na-tion, he's the smart-est. A
(Oo, oo, oo, oo, oo, oo. Oo,

Ro-bert Wil-liams stroke__ and splat-ter, I at-test__ to your__ gray mat-ter.
oo.

Liv-ing kings,__ how true it rings, these are just a few of my fa-vor-ite things.__
Oo, oo, oo, oo, oo, oo. Oo,

oo.

Bridge

Good God,__ where's my sleigh__ now? Good God, play-ing for days__ now.

Good God, well, an - y day___ now.___ Good God, ___ take me a - way___ now.

Good God, ___ De - Nir - o's in - sane___ now. Good God, ___ rack - in' my brains___ now.

Good God, well, an - y day___ now.___ Good God, ___ take me a - way___ now.___

Guitar Solo

G9   G♭9   F9sus4   N.C.   N.C.(B5)

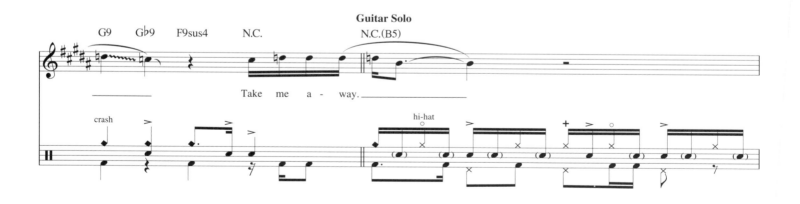

___ Take me a - way.___

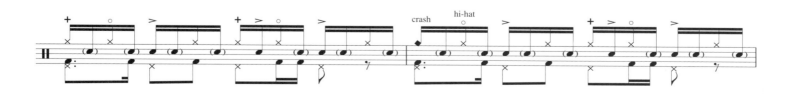

Verse

N.C.(B7)

2. Me and my friends and the sex ma - chine,

do un - to oth - ers like my broth - er Bean.__ I know you've got a moth - er, so give her a hug,__ I

know you've got a moth - er with a whole lot of love.__ Bil - ly sings and Ba - sie swings,__

these are just a few of my fa - vor - ite things.__

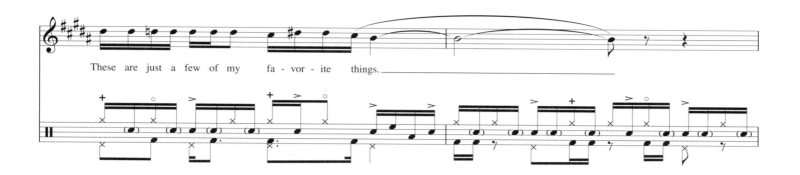

These are just a few of my fa - vor - ite things._____

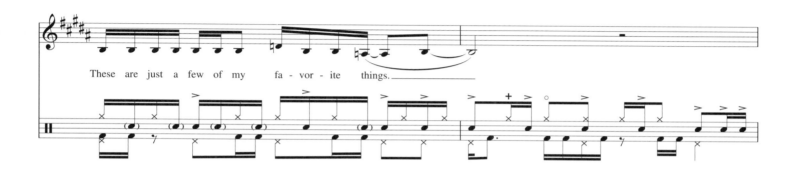

These are just a few of my fa - vor - ite things._____

Outro
N.C.

These are just a few.____ Whoa!

from *By the Way*

Minor Thing

Words and Music by Anthony Kiedis, Flea, John Frusciante and Chad Smith

from *One Hot Minute*
My Friends

Words and Music by Anthony Kiedis, Flea, Chad Smith and David Navarro

90

Seque to "Coffee Shop"

from *Mother's Milk*

Nobody Weird Like Me

Words and Music by Anthony Kiedis, Flea, John Frusciante and Chad Smith

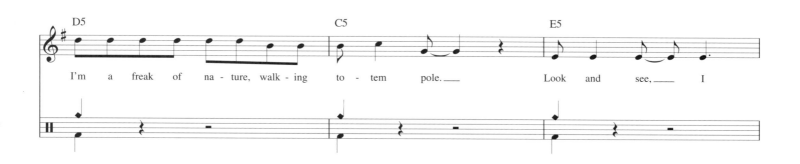

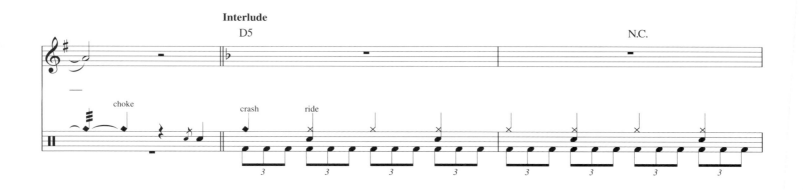

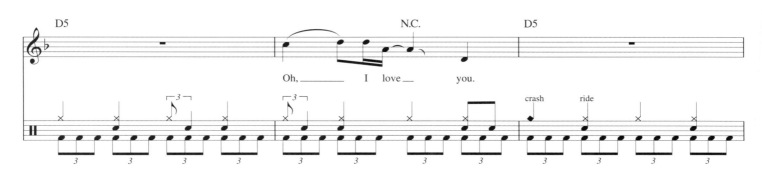

Free Time

Fade out

100

from *One Hot Minute*

One Big Mob

Words and Music by Anthony Kiedis, Flea, Chad Smith and David Navarro

ev - 'ry-thing you ev - er see is nev - er more than you and me. Give it on in to the beau-ty of the mys-ter - y. ____
rock-in' to the beat of a kan - ga - roo? Let me kiss your feet and fore - head too. ____

Interlude
Half-time feel

(B5) (A) Bm (E5) (D5)

(One big mob is...) (Ah.)

mf

crash hi-hat crash | crash ride crash ride | crash ride | crash ride

Bm (E5) (D5)

crash ride crash ride | crash | crash ride

Bm E D5

One big mob is one ____ big home, _ a bro-ken home. ____

crash ride hi-hat ride crash ride

Bm E D5

I'd like to share some air ____ with you, _ some air with you. ____

crash ride hi-hat ride crash ride

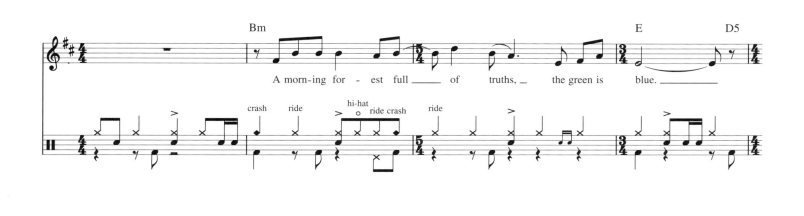

A morn-ing for - est full _____ of truths, ___ the green is blue. _____

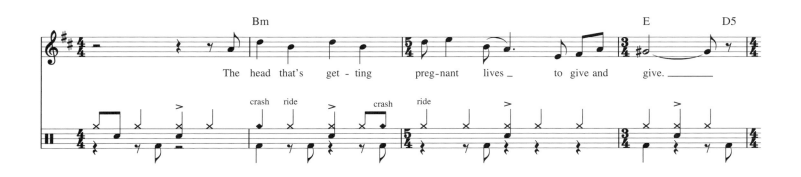

The head that's get - ting preg-nant lives _ to give and give. _____

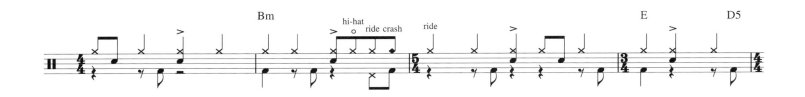

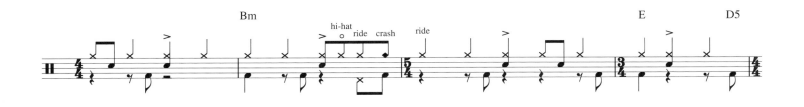

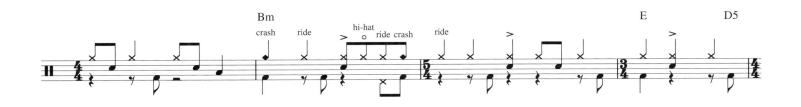

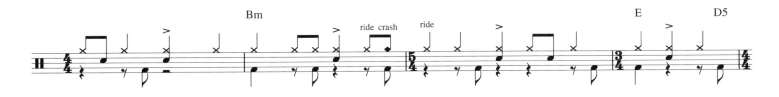

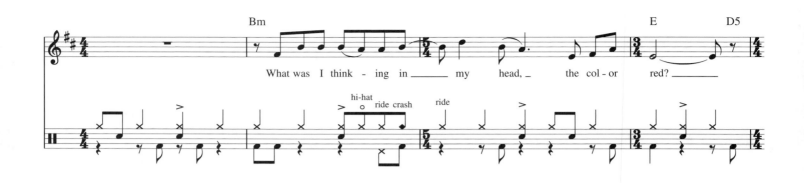

What was I think-ing in _____ my head, _ the col-or red? _____

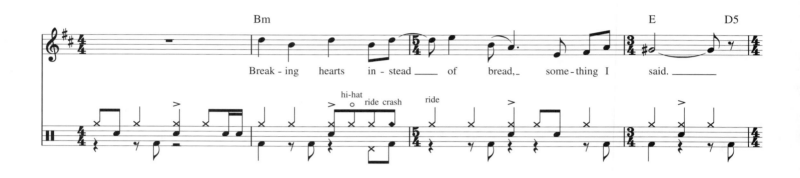

Break-ing hearts in-stead _____ of bread, _ some-thing I said. _____

Check-mat-ed by frus-tra - tion, I _____ need to be cut _____ loose. _

_____ A dif-'rent kind of be-ing lost,_ a sul-len cost. _____

*Play 3 times

* Grad. cresc.

End half-time feel

Bridge

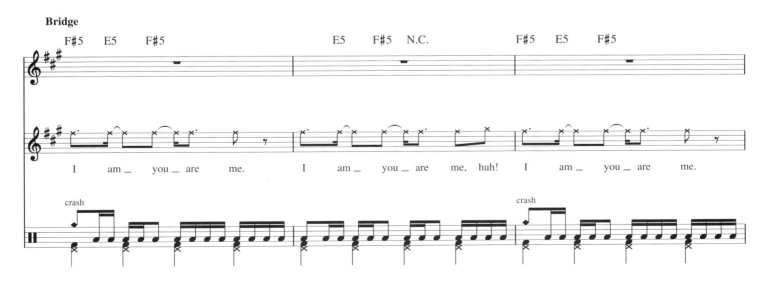

I am __ you __ are me.   I am __ you __ are me, huh!   I am __ you __ are me.

from *Californication*

Right on Time

Words and Music by Anthony Kiedis, Flea, John Frusciante and Chad Smith

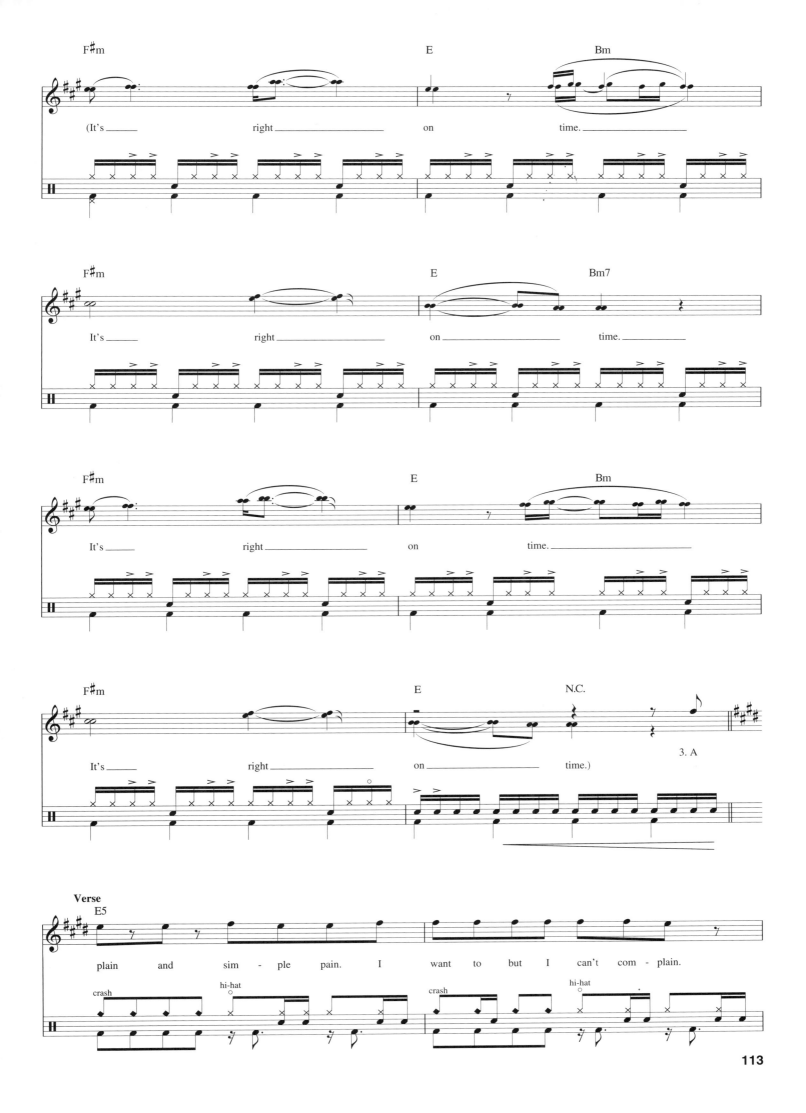

(It's _____ right _____ on _____ time. _____)

It's _____ right _____ on _____ time. _____

It's _____ right _____ on _____ time. _____

It's _____ right _____ on _____ time.)

3. A

Verse

plain and sim - ple pain. I want to but I can't com - plain.

crash   hi-hat   crash   hi-hat

Death row, let's us go. It's time to blow up for the show.

All the world re - ver - ber - a - ted. Com - ing through we mo - tor - ca - ted.

Vi - brate when we op - er - a - ted. Turn - ing up in sol - ed sta - ted.

C#m E B F#m

C#m E B F#m

C#m E B F#m

C#m E B F#m E5

Oh, Lord.

Scar Tissue

Words and Music by Anthony Kiedis, Flea, John Frusciante and Chad Smith

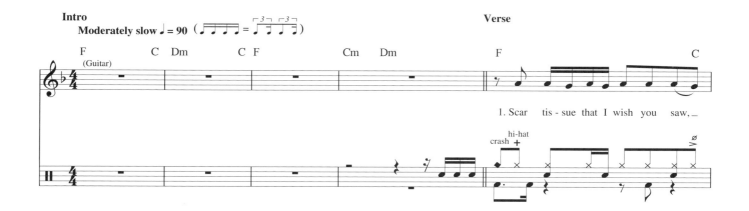

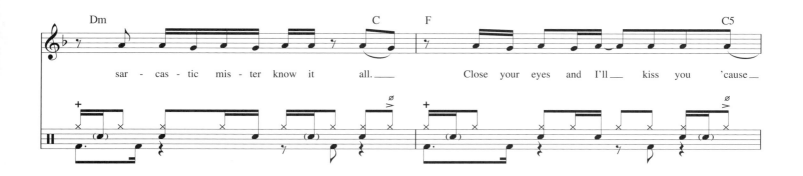

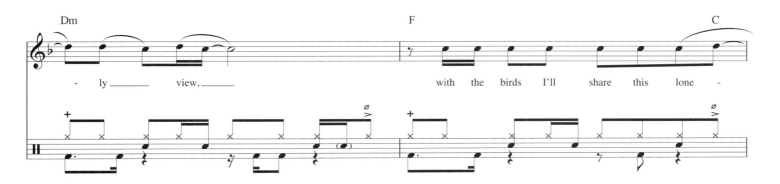

Interlude

- ly   view. _____
- ly...)

crash hi-hat

Verse

3. Blood   loss   in   a   bath - room   stall,

crash hi-hat

south - ern   girl   with   a   scar - let   drawl.   Wave   good - bye ___ to   ma   and   pa   'cause ___

Chorus

___   with   the   birds   I'll   share, ___   with   the   birds   I'll   share   this   lone -
                                                                (Share ___ this   lone -

crash hi-hat

from *By the Way*

Throw Away Your Television

Words and Music by Anthony Kiedis, Flea, John Frusciante and Chad Smith

126

from *What Hits!?*

True Men Don't Kill Coyotes

Words and Music by Flea, Anthony Kiedis, Cliff Martinez and Jack Sherman

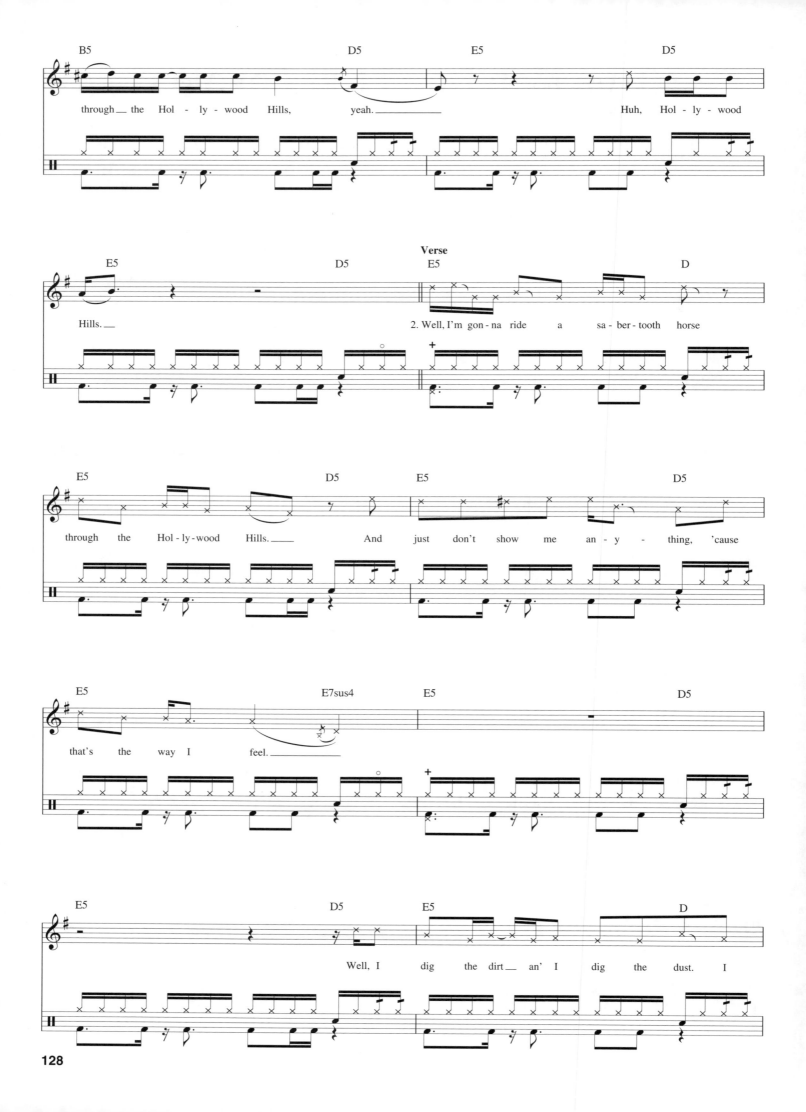

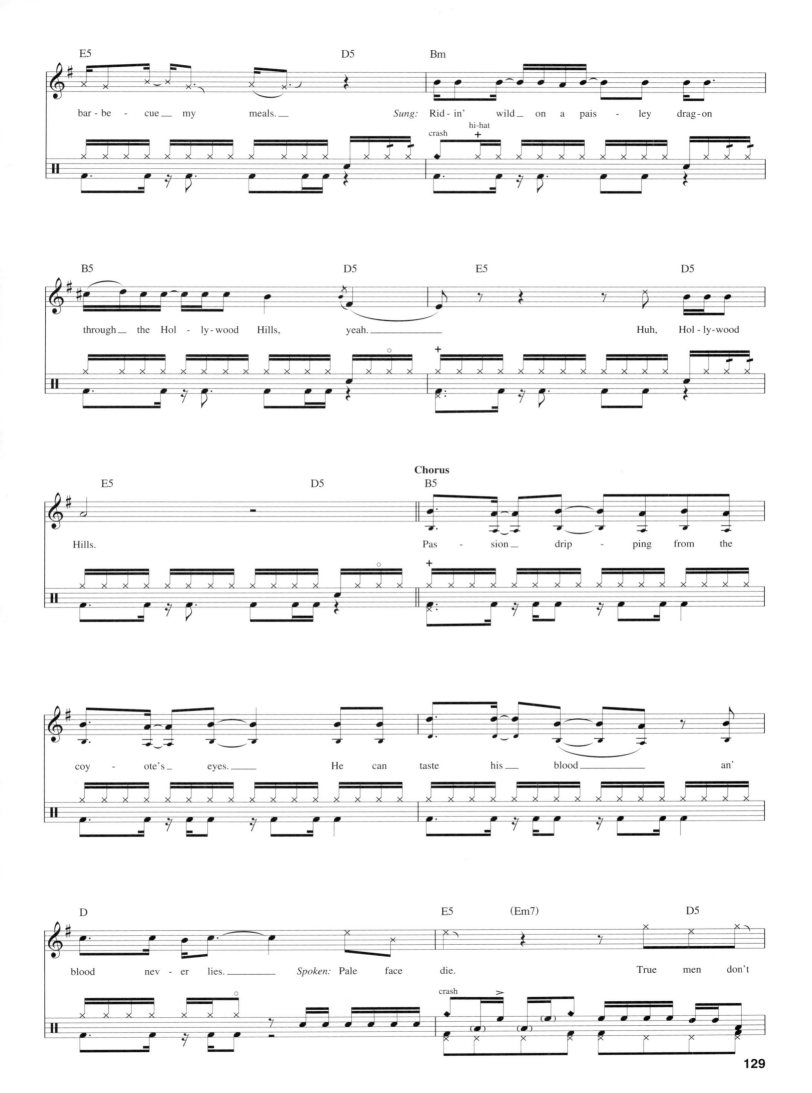

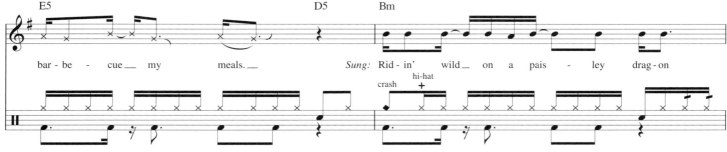

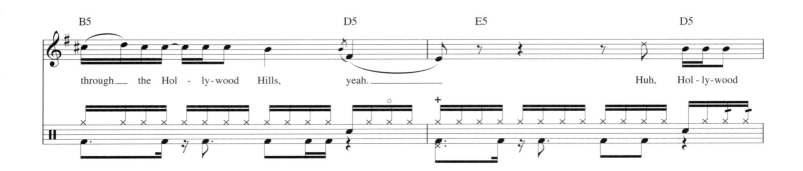

Chorus

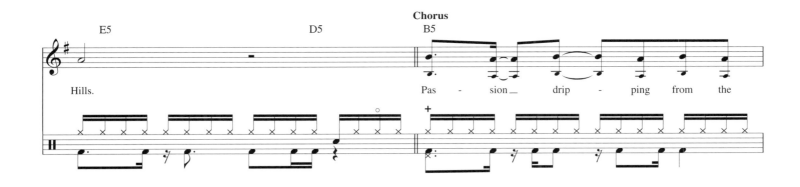

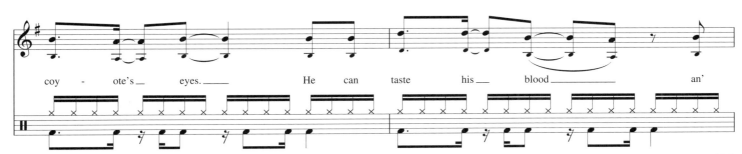

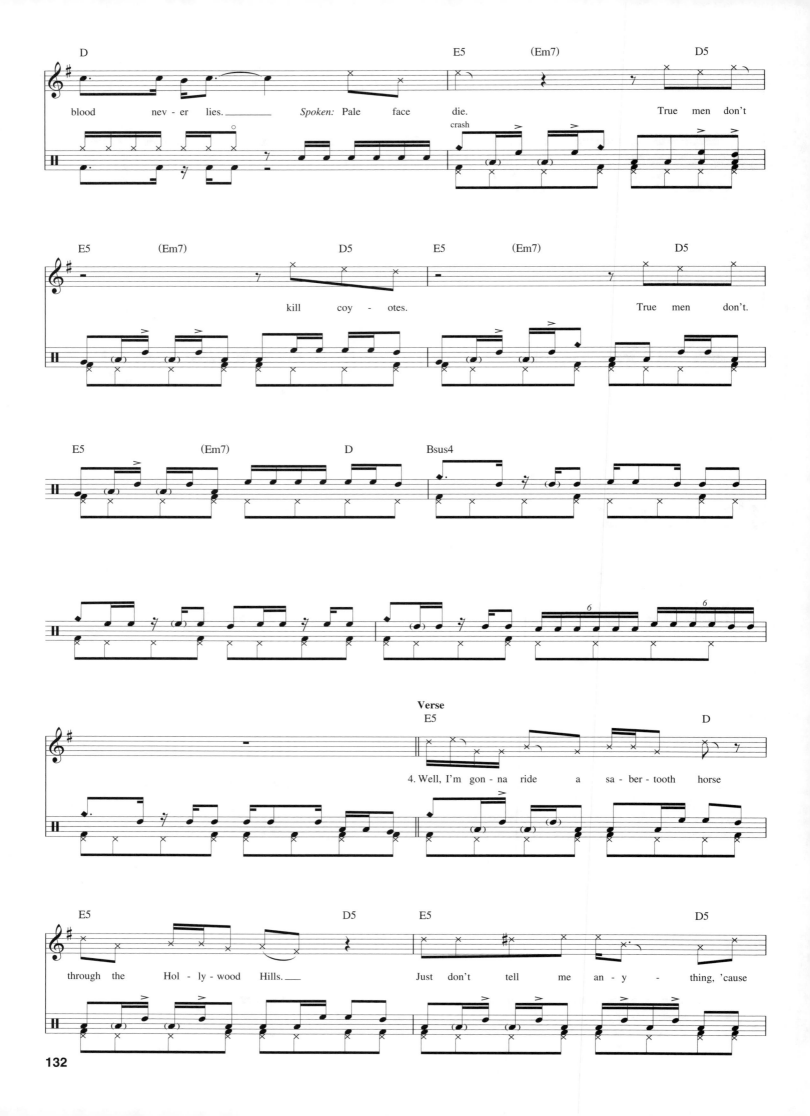

blood nev-er lies._____ *Spoken:* Pale face die.

crash

True men don't

kill coy - otes.

True men don't.

Verse

4. Well, I'm gon - na ride a sa - ber - tooth horse

through the Hol - ly - wood Hills.___ Just don't tell me an - y - thing, 'cause

132

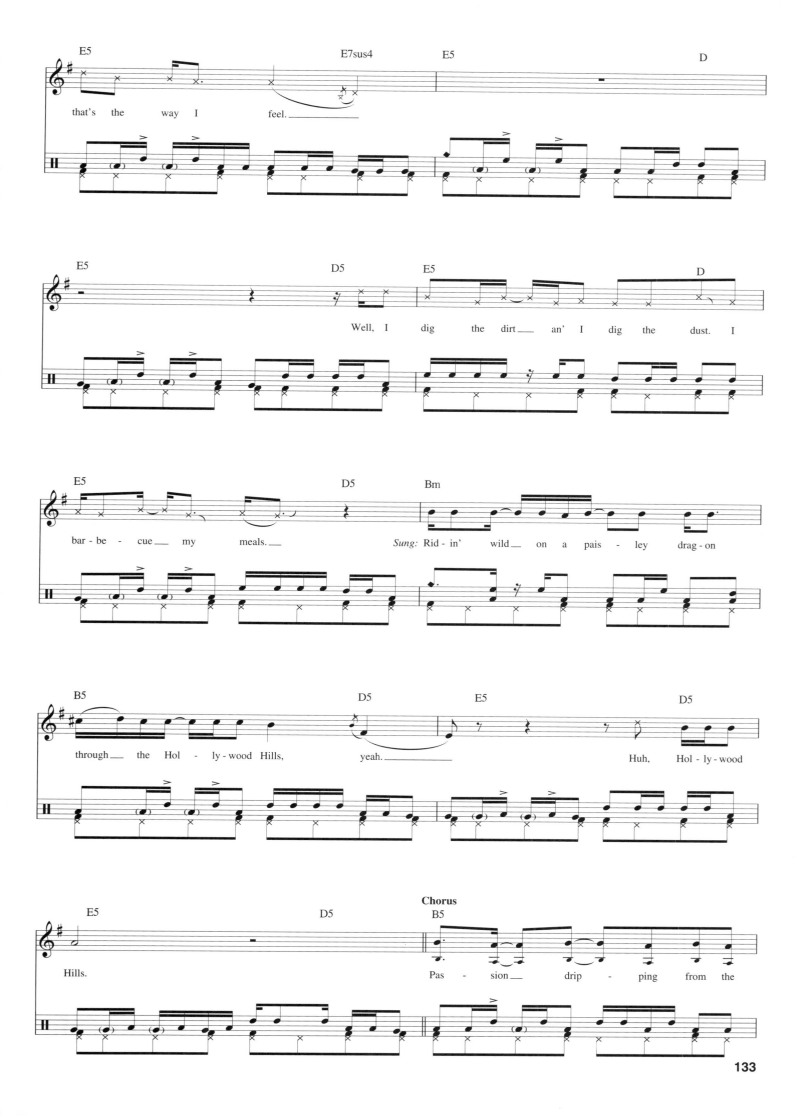

coy - ote's ___ eyes. ___ He can taste his ___ blood _____ an'

blood nev - er lies. ___ *Spoken:* Pale face die. True men don't

kill coy - otes. True men don't.

True men don't

from *Blood Sugar Sex Magik*

Under the Bridge

Words and Music by Anthony Kiedis, Flea, John Frusciante and Chad Smith

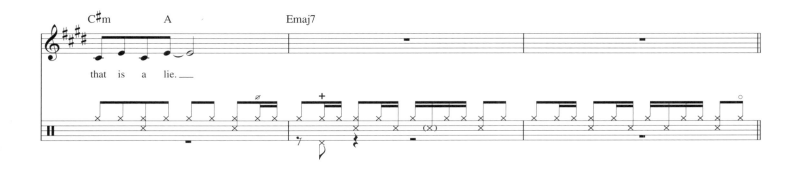

Pre-Chorus

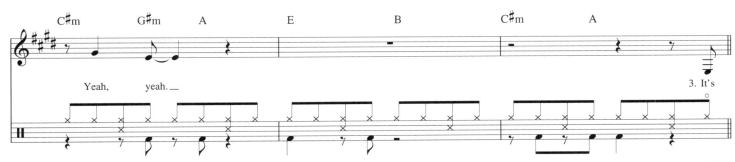

137

Drum Notation Legend

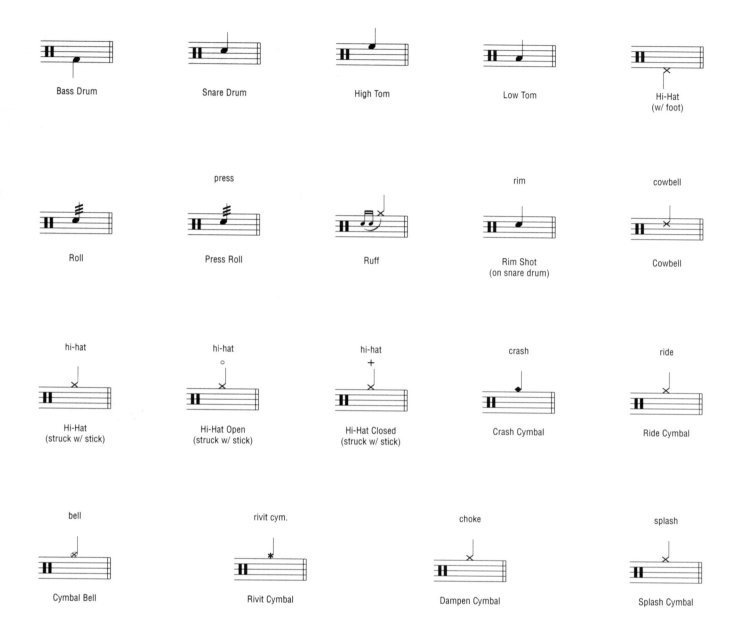

DRUM RECORDED VERSIONS
FROM HAL LEONARD

LEARN TO PLAY THE DRUMSET – BOOK 1

by Peter Magadini

This unique method starts students out on the entire drumset and teaches them the basics in the shortest amount of time. Book 1 covers basic 4- and 5-piece set-ups, grips and sticks, reading and improvisation, coordination of hands and feet, and features a variety of contemporary and basic rhythm patterns with exercise breakdowns for each.
06620030 Book/CD Pack $14.95

CREATIVE TIMEKEEPING FOR THE CONTEMPORARY JAZZ DRUMMER

by Rick Mattingly

Combining a variety of jazz ride cymbal patterns with coordination and reading exercises, *Creative Timekeeping* develops true independence: the ability to play any rhythm on the ride cymbal while playing any rhythm on the snare and bass drums. It provides a variety of jazz ride cymbal patterns as well as coordination and reading exercises that can be played along with them. Five chapters: Ride Cymbal Patterns; Coordination Patterns and Reading; Combination Patterns and Reading; Applications; and Cymbal Reading.
06621764 . . . . $8.95

THE DRUMSET MUSICIAN

by Rod Morgenstein and Rick Mattingly

Containing hundreds of practical, usable beats and fills, *The Drumset Musician* teaches you how to apply a variety of patterns and grooves to the actual performance of songs. The accompanying CD includes demos as well as 14 play-along tracks covering a wide range of rock, blues and pop styles, with detailed instructions on how to create exciting, solid drum parts.
06620011 Book/CD Pack $19.95

THE TECHNO PRIMER

THE ESSENTIAL REFERENCE FOR LOOP-BASED MUSIC STYLES

by Tony Verderosa

This book/CD pack contains an enhanced CD with techno music tracks in a variety of styles – as well as video clips and a demo version of the ACID™ XPress program by Sonic Foundry®, a history of electronic music, and a detailed guide to techno styles. Also includes information on interactive music on the web, digital recording via the internet, understanding MIDI, the art of sound design, the DJ drummer concept and more.
00330543 Book/CD Pack $19.95

40 INTERMEDIATE SNARE DRUM SOLOS

FOR CONCERT PERFORMANCE

by Ben Hans

This book provides the advancing percussionist with interesting solo material in all musical styles. It is designed as a lesson supplement, or as performance material for recitals and solo competitions. Includes: 40 intermediate snare drum solos presented in easy-to-read notation; a music glossary; Percussive Arts Society rudiment chart; suggested sticking, dynamics and articulation markings; and much more!
06620067 . . . . $7.95

YOU CAN'T BEAT OUR DRUM BOOKS!

FOR MORE INFORMATION, SEE YOUR LOCAL MUSIC DEALER, OR WRITE TO:

HAL•LEONARD®
CORPORATION
7777 W. BLUEMOUND RD. P.O. BOX 13819
MILWAUKEE, WISCONSIN 53213

Visit Hal Leonard online at **www.halleonard.com**
Prices, contents, and availability subject to change without notice.

STUDIES IN SOLO PERCUSSION

by Morris Goldenberg

For intermediate-to-advanced percussionists, this book is designed to assist the solo player in combining groups of instruments cumulatively. Instruments include the snare drum, bass drum, tenor drum, field drum, piccolo, temple block, cowbell, bongos, tom-tom, wood block, and many more. The book starts off with seven studies for two drums, moves to three studies for three drums, and ends with sixteen studies for four or more instruments.
00347779 . . . . $7.50

THE DRUMMER'S ALMANAC

by Jon Cohan

This celebration of the art of drumming is a must-have for all drummers, beginning to advanced. With essential tips on techniques and tongue-in-cheek anecdotes, *The Drummer's Almanac* is very informative and very fun. Includes lots of photographs, interviews with legendary Yamaha drum endorsees, quotes, jokes, helpful hints, and more. Chapters include: A Short History of the Drum Set; 40 Rudiments You Should Know; 20 Grooves to Get You Through Any Gig; How I Got The Gig; Gigs from Hell; Drummers' Favorite Drummers; Drummers' Best Excuses and Other Jokes; Drum Tuning Tips; Drum Repair and Maintenance; and more.
00330237 . . . . $12.95

INSTANT GUIDE TO DRUM GROOVES

THE ESSENTIAL REFERENCE FOR THE WORKING DRUMMER

by Maria Martinez

Become a more versatile drumset player! From traditional Dixieland to cutting-edge hip-hop, *Instant Guide to Drum Grooves* is a handy source featuring 100 patterns that will prepare working drummers for the stylistic variety of modern gigs. The book includes essential beats and grooves in such styles as: jazz, shuffle, country, rock, funk, New Orleans, reggae, calypso, Brazilian and Latin.
06620056 Book/CD Pack $9.95

THE COMPLETE DRUMSET RUDIMENTS

by Peter Magadini

Use your imagination to incorporate these rudimental etudes into new patterns that you can apply to the drumset or tom toms as you develop your hand technique with the Snare Drum Rudiments, your hand and foot technique with the Drumset Rudiments and your polyrhythmic technique with the Polyrhythm Rudiments. Adopt them all into your own creative expressions based on ideas you come up with while practicing.
06620016 Book/CD Pack $14.95

DRUM TUNING

THE ULTIMATE GUIDE

by Scott Schroedl

This book/CD pack is designed for drummers of all styles and levels. It contains step-by-step instruction along with over 35 professional photos that allow you to see the tools and tuning techniques up close. Covers: preparation; drumhead basics; drum construction and head properties; tom-toms; snare drum; bassdrum; the drum set as one instrument; drum sounds and tuning over the years; when to change heads; and more.
06620060 Book/CD Pack $12.95

Transcribed Scores are vocal and instrumental arrangements of music from some of the greatest groups in music. These excellent publications feature transcribed parts for lead vocals, lead guitar, rhythm, guitar, bass, drums, and all of the various instruments used in each specific recording session. All songs are arranged exactly the way the artists recorded them.

00672463	Aerosmith – Big Ones	$24.95
00673228	The Beatles – Complete Scores (Boxed Set)	$75.00
00672378	The Beatles – Transcribed Scores	$24.95
00672459	George Benson Collection	$24.95
00673208	Best of Blood, Sweat & Tears	$19.95
00672367	Chicago – Volume 1	$24.95
00672368	Chicago – Volume 2	$24.95
00672460	Miles Davis – Kind of Blue (Sketch Scores)	$19.95
00672490	Miles Davis – Kind of Blue (Hardcover)	$29.95
00672502	Deep Purple – Greatest Hits	$24.95
00672333	Jack DeJohnette Collection	$19.95
00672327	Gil Evans Collection	$24.95
00672508	Ben Folds – Rockin' the Suburbs	$19.95
00672427	Ben Folds Five – Selections from Naked Baby Photos	$19.95
00672458	Ben Folds Five – The Unauthorized Biography of Reinhold Messner	$19.95
00672428	Ben Folds Five – Whatever and Ever, Amen	$19.95
00672399	Foo Fighters	$24.95
00672442	Foo Fighters – The Colour and the Shape	$24.95
00672477	Foo Fighters – There Is Nothing Left to Lose	$24.95
00672472	Goo Goo Dolls Collection	$24.95
00672313	Jimi Hendrix – Band of Gypsys	$29.95
00672311	Jimi Hendrix – Electric Ladyland	$29.95
00672397	Jimi Hendrix – Experience Hendrix	$29.95
00672500	Best of Incubus	$24.95
00672469	Billy Joel Collection	$24.95
00672415	Eric Johnson – Ah Via Musicom	$24.95
00672414	Eric Johnson – Tones	$24.95

00672417	Eric Johnson – Venus Isle	$24.95
00672470	Carole King – Greatest Hits	$24.95
00672499	John Lennon – Greatest Hits	$24.95
00672465	John Lennon – Imagine	$24.95
00672478	The Best of Megadeth	$24.95
00672409	Megadeth – Rust in Peace	$24.95
00690582	Nickel Creek – Nickel Creek	$19.95
00690586	Nickel Creek – This Side	$19.95
00672424	Nirvana – Bleach	$24.95
00672421	Nirvana – From the Muddy Banks of the Wishkah	$24.95
00672403	Nirvana – In Utero	$24.95
00672404	Nirvana – Incesticide	$24.95
00672402	Nirvana – Nevermind	$24.95
00672405	Nirvana – Unplugged in New York	$24.95
00672466	The Offspring – Americana	$24.95
00672400	Red Hot Chili Peppers – Blood Sugar Sex Magik	$24.95
00672456	Red Hot Chili Peppers – Californication	$24.95
00672422	Red Hot Chili Peppers – Mother's Milk	$24.95
00672358	Red Hot Chili Peppers – One Hot Minute	$27.95
00672467	Red Hot Chili Peppers – What Hits!?	$24.95
00672408	Rolling Stones – Exile on Main Street	$24.95
00672360	Santana's Greatest Hits	$26.95
00675170	The Best of Spyro Gyra	$18.95
00672468	Sting – Fields of Gold	$24.95
00674655	Sting – Nothing Like the Sun	$19.95
00673230	Sting – Ten Summoner's Tales	$19.95
00675520	Best of Weather Report	$18.95
00675800	Yellow Jackets – Four Corners	$18.95

Prices and availability subject to change